Willie O'Ree

Praise for Willie O'Ree

"[Mortillaro's] touch is light and energetic, so that O'Ree's life story advances quickly . . . I would highly recommend this book for literacy collections, classroom libraries, and general libraries. It could also make a nice gift for young hockey fans. Rated E, excellent, enduring, everyone should see it!"

— *Resource Links*

"Willie O'Ree is well-researched. [Mortillaro] has made Willie O'Ree's story an engrossing one. Her writing style is easy to read and suitable for young readers. Highly Recommended."

— *Canadian Review of Materials*

"[Mortillaro] does paint clear pictures of the sport's history and significance, especially in Canada, as well as the racial hostility that O'Ree braved through much of his playing career."

— *Booklist*

"This biography stands on its own as a well written life story of a man who had his fifteen minutes of fame but supplements the Willie O'Ree story with a running anecdote of racism in society and modern sports, physical impairment, the history of the development of the NHL, the civil rights movement in the 1950s and 60s. Willie O'Ree is a gem to be discovered."

— Canadian Teacher

Also by Nicole Mortillaro in the Lorimer Recordbooks
    series:
Jarome Iginla: How the NHL's first black captain gives back
*Something to Prove: The story of hockey tough guy Bobby
    Clarke*

Willie O'Ree

*The story of the first
black player in the NHL*

Nicole Mortillaro

James Lorimer & Company Ltd., Publishers
Toronto

James Lorimer & Company Ltd., Publishers acknowledges funding support from
the Ontario Arts Council (OAC), an agency of the Government of Ontario. We
acknowledge the support of the Canada Council for the Arts, which last year
invested $153 million to bring the arts to Canadians throughout the country. This
project has been made possible in part by the Government of Canada and with the
support of the Ontario Media Development Corporation.

Cover design: Meredith Bangay
Cover images: courtesy of Nova Scotia Archives (top) and the Hockey Hall of
Fame (bottom)

978-1-4594-1304-7
eBook also available 978-1-4594-0197-6

Cataloguing data available from Library and Archives Canada.

Published by: Distributed in the US by:
James Lorimer & Company Ltd., Publishers   Lerner Publisher Services
117 Peter Street, Suite 304   1251 Washington Ave N
Toronto, ON, Canada   Minneapolis, MN, USA
M5V 0M3   55401
www.lorimer.ca   www.lernerbooks.com

Printed and bound in Canada.
Manufactured by Friesens Corporation in Altona, Manitoba,
Canada in April 2018.
Job # 242780

To my angel Sara:
Don't ever let anything stop you
from doing what you love.

"You never fail until you stop trying."
— Willie O'Ree

Contents

Prologue

The sun peeks out from the clouds on Saint Catherine Street West. Pedestrians are bundled against the cold. They pass the Montreal Forum, their chilly breath hanging in the air. Snowbanks line the streets. It is January 18, 1958. Tonight the Montreal Canadiens will battle it out against the Boston Bruins. It's sure to be another good hockey game between these two rivals.

There is nothing unusual or special

about this day to most people . . . at least not outside the Forum doors.

Inside this hallowed hockey building is another story.

Willie O'Ree is suiting up to play for the Boston Bruins. Just last week, he was in that dressing room as a member of the Quebec Aces. But it feels different to dress for an NHL game for the first time — and against his heroes.

For Willie, it is more than just the thrill of playing in the NHL. Willie is playing against the oldest and most successful team, the Montreal Canadiens. And it is his favourite team. They have already won the Stanley Cup nine times — three in the last three years. Montreal is home to his hockey heroes, such as Maurice Richard, Henri Richard, Jean Béliveau, "Boom Boom" Geoffrion, and Jacques Plante. It is like a dream to him.

When Willie was 14, he decided to try

to make it to the NHL — and he has done it. Twenty-three-year-old Willie is suiting up with the Boston Bruins, playing against one of his favourite teams. It doesn't get much better than that.

"Just go out and play the game," Willie's coach Milt Schmidt tells him. Willie takes comfort in Schmidt's words.

But it's hard for Willie *not* to be nervous.

Tonight, the Bruins win the game. Not much is made of O'Ree's historic appearance at the Forum. Montreal fans are mostly disappointed with their team's loss, especially against the Bruins.

After the game, Willie is interviewed by Gordon Sinclair Jr.

"It must be an exciting thing, isn't it, to get in an NHL game for the Boston Bruins. How do you feel about it, Willie? Anything unusual?" he asks.

"No. It was the greatest thrill of my life,

I believe. I'll always remember this day," Willie says.

"I'm going to ask you a question. I think in the first period, you looked like you were a little nervous. Were you?"

"Yes," Willie chuckles. "A bit."

"It scared you a little?"

"Yes, it did," he says happily. "But after a few minutes, I relaxed and became myself again."

Willie O'Ree has made it all the way to the big time. Like the hockey stars he is playing with and against, he has worked hard and stayed strong to see his dream come true. And he has done something even greater. Willie O'Ree is the first black man to ever play in the NHL.

1 Black Ice

Where hockey got its start is a thing that hockey experts and fans love to debate. It was Kingston, Ontario. It was Nova Scotia. Maybe hockey wasn't invented in Canada at all. Maybe it was Russia.

No matter where it was invented, the game we love, the game that defines us as Canadians, has become a part of us.

When hockey first appeared, it was enjoyed by people of high society. Still, you could find people of all backgrounds playing on ponds across Canada. And it wasn't just for the white faces of the British and French.

Hockey was loved by the blacks that had come to Canada through the slave trade. Black people had not gained full equality in Canada. But they had progressed much further than their neighbours in the United States. They were no longer enslaved. They could buy and live freely, though not without facing racism of their own.

Hockey was hugely popular across the country, and it soon became very popular in the black community. In the 1880s, baseball was very popular in Nova Scotia. Clubs had popped up across the province. In the winter, these players would turn to hockey. In 1894, the first black hockey league was formed. One of its founders was 26-year-old Henry Sylvester Williams. Williams had settled in Halifax and attended Dalhousie University

God and Hockey

In the black community, the birth of organized hockey was partnered with religion. It was organized by Baptists; their rule book was the Bible. And though the church involvement might seem strange today, at that time, it helped unite a people who wanted equality with the whites in Canada. It was a unifying force.

Law School. He and the black Baptist church promoted two hockey teams, the Halifax Eurekas and the Halifax Stanley. Soon the Colored Hockey League was formed. Additional teams were born: the Dartmouth Jubilees, the Hammond Plains Moss Backs, the Africville Sea-Sides.

Many of the team names had special meaning for black players and fans. It might seem that the Jubilees took their name from the Jubilee celebrations of Queen Victoria's reign. But to the black community, it

Players from the Colored Hockey League of the Maritimes

represented a time of emancipation, when the queen had declared slave trade illegal in the British Empire. To the black community, the word *eureka* referred to those who had found God. The name of the Africville Sea-Sides (which would be spelled "seasides" by the white media) meant more than being near the ocean. People who helped slaves escape to Canada were called "slave stealers." They

Blacks in Canada

The first slave brought from Africa to New France might have been Olivier Le Jeune. He was sold in 1629 in Quebec, but was buried as a servant, leading some to believe that he died a free man. By 1759, there was a total of 3,604 slaves in New France. Under British rule, 2,000 more slaves were brought to the New World. However, 3,500 free blacks came from England at the same time, many settling in Nova Scotia and New Brunswick. On August 28, 1833, British Parliament passed a law abolishing slavery in all British colonies.

risked their lives by helping escaped slaves, sometimes being beaten or even killed. The ones who lived would have the mark "SS" burned into their right hand or face. The Sea-Sides proudly wore the "SS" on their uniforms, which for them stood for "slave salvation."

So was born the game of hockey in

the black community. The Colored Hockey League saw some time of success. Black players faced off against their white counterparts and were evenly matched. Within their own league, competition was fierce.

Soon league games were being reported in newspapers. But it wasn't always a good report. An article in *The Halifax Herald* reported on a game between the Jubilees and the Stanley. It compared the game to the struggle of the blacks against slavery. As noted in *Black Ice: The Lost History of the Colored Hockey League of the Maritimes, 1895–1925*, the article prompted a letter to the editor, chastising the paper for blatant racism: "It started off with some degree of truth, but really did not last long in that strain, but manufactured the greatest bunch of falsehoods, trash and insults to respectable readers." The letter was clearly written by an educated black man. This sent the white community into an uproar. Who would dare to speak out? Who would suggest that the white community was ignorant? It was assumed that it was a man named Henry Williams. He fled from Canada, finally settling in England.

Sadly, the Colored Hockey League continued to face racism. People feared that somehow blacks would gain power through sport. The league folded shortly after World War I. And blacks would remain shut out of hockey for more than 30 years.

2 Life in New Brunswick

The moment three-year-old Willie O'Ree stepped onto the ice, he fell in love with it. He wore training skates: two blocks of wood with double blades on the bottom and straps that slipped on over his shoes. He learned to skate in his backyard. There he could skate as long as he wanted. There he was free. And it didn't matter that he wasn't fast: he soon would be.

"We had a pretty good-sized backyard, and my dad would flood the backyard and there was an instant rink . . . I remember pushing a chair around the rink," Willie says.

Willie was born on October 15, 1935, and grew up in Fredericton, New Brunswick. New Brunswick is the third-smallest province in Canada, but to Willie, it was huge. It was dotted with lakes that made for great skating. And Fredericton winters were cold. But Willie didn't mind. Cold ice was fast ice.

"There were four outdoor rinks within 15 minutes of where I lived . . . and then there was the river and ponds and lakes and creeks," Willie remembers.

By the time he was five, Willie was playing hockey with his brother Richard and other neighbourhood kids. And he had a deep love of the game. Hockey made him feel alive.

"I loved the feel of the wind rushing by as I flew along the ice . . . I loved

Queen Street, Fredericton, 1940

having the puck on my stick and learning how to stickhandle," Willie writes in his book, *The Autobiography of Willie O'Ree: Hockey's Black Pioneer.* "The speed that I could reach on my skates when I was stickhandling with the puck was like defying gravity."

But Willie and Richard weren't like the rest of their friends who played. The O'Rees were black.

The family lived on Charlotte Street.

The O'Rees were one of only two black families in the whole town. The other black family lived just down the street. There were other blacks living on the outskirts of town, but in town, it was just the O'Rees and the Lawrences. The Lawrence boys grew up and moved on, leaving Willie and his brothers and sisters the only black children in the city.

But if there was racism in Fredericton or Canada, Willie didn't see it. "When I was a little boy, all I knew was that hockey WAS my life, and that 'black' meant the puck, and 'white' meant the ice," he writes.

Willie was one of thirteen children born to Rosebud and Harry Douglas O'Ree. His grandparents had come to Canada by the Underground Railroad, fleeing slavery. Harry worked for the city of Fredericton doing road maintenance. His mother worked hard raising her children and taking care of the home. The whole family was active, his brothers and sisters playing various sports. They liked to keep busy.

Life around the O'Ree house was typical of the time. Willie had chores, like catching and killing chickens for dinner and tending the family's garden.

"That's another reason I loved winter so much. Not only was I able to play hockey every day, but I didn't have to weed that garden!" Willie says.

Back in the 1940s, hockey games were played on outdoor rinks. And it was cold — really cold. Snow would be piled high around the rink. Fans would stand on them to watch the games, jumping up and down to keep warm. On those days, Willie tried extra hard to impress his parents.

Willie used skating as part of his school life: whenever he could, he'd skate to

The Underground Railroad

Between 1840 and 1860, many slaves from the southern United States, where slavery was still legal, headed north. They used the Underground Railroad, a network of secret passages, safe houses, and people who helped get escaped slaves to Canada. The journey was a dangerous one. Getting caught could mean death. Places had code names so the route was secret. For example, Detroit was called Midnight. The Detroit River was called Jordan, a river in the Bible that was said to lead to the Promised Land. For escaped slaves, the Promised Land was Canada, where slavery had been abolished. It is believed that 30,000 escaped slaves made it to Canada.

school. And he'd count the hours until he could put those skates back on and skate home.

Education was very important to Willie's parents. And, unlike a lot of children, Willie loved school. He even loved having homework. He was good at math and social studies. But there was one thing he hated: spelling. And he came up with ways to avoid it. "I would do anything to try to miss those spelling tests. I'd say that I had lost my spelling book in a snowbank and had to wait for the spring thaw before I could find it again."

When he was 14, Willie started playing organized hockey with his older brother Richard, who was in his 20s.

Sometimes Richard would hit him hard and Willie would complain. "He'd say, 'You're going to get hit, so you'd better learn how to get hit,'" Willie says.

Willie tried out for his school hockey team. One day he gave a clean check to his coach's son. The hit broke the young man's collarbone. The coach kicked Willie off the team.

That didn't stop Willie. He went on

to play in the New Brunswick Hockey League for the Fredericton Junior Capitals, and then for the Capitals in the senior league. Guess who wanted Willie back after his success with the Capitals? When Willie's high-school coach contacted Willie to come back to the team, Willie turned him down.

All the while Willie played hockey, racism was silent, but it still existed. There were places in town that he couldn't go. There may not have been any signs posted, but it was an unspoken rule. He didn't let it bother him . . . until he needed a haircut.

Five houses down the road from the O'Rees lived barber Joe McQuade and his family. Mr. McQuade would cut Willie's hair on his porch. But 13-year-old Willie became curious. He asked McQuade what would happen if he went into McQuade's barber shop to get his hair cut. McQuade thought about it and finally said that he didn't know. So Willie told him he would come to the shop for a haircut.

The day came and Willie walked into the barber shop. It was busy and there were people waiting. Heads turned. McQuade was busy with a customer. When another barber looked at him, Willie told him he was waiting for Mr. McQuade. There was silence as Willie sat down. Would something be said? Would he be asked to leave?

Finally, his turn came and McQuade took Willie to his chair. From that day on, Willie always went to his barber shop for a haircut.

It was Willie's first stand against racism. And it wouldn't be his last.

3 Baseball Hero

The O'Rees were an athletic family. Willie's brothers and sisters were into many sports. Willie played about nine different sports in all. He loved football and was very good at baseball. Willie played shortstop and second base for Little League teams growing up. Willie credits some of his baseball skills to his father. He loved everything about the summertime sport: the smell of the grass, the smell of oiled baseball gloves, and, of course, summer itself.

In 1948, when Willie was 13, his baseball team won Fredericton's Bantam city championship. As part of their reward, the West Enders won a trip to New York — the Big Apple.

New York was home to two baseball teams: the New York Yankees and the Brooklyn Dodgers. The Yankees were the giants of the game, made famous by Babe Ruth, the homerun giant. By the time Willie was visiting, they'd won the championship 11 times (and would go on to win it again that fall).

But for Willie, it wasn't about the Yankees. It was all about the Dodgers. After all, the Dodgers were home to the biggest giant of them all: Jackie Robinson.

Jackie Robinson had broken down barriers. He was the first black man to play in Major League Baseball (MLB). It wasn't that blacks hadn't played baseball before. There had been Negro leagues for many years. But a black man playing with and against white men? That was unheard of.

Robinson was no stranger to racism. When he was in the army, he was ordered to the back of the bus. Robinson would have none of it. He was even charged in military court for it. Robinson was a fighter.

And then he met Dodgers president Branch Rickey. Rickey knew Robinson was talented. But he also worried that he was a fighter. According to Larry Schwartz of ESPN, their conversation in 1945 went something like this:

> Rickey: *I know you're a good ballplayer. What I don't know is whether you have the guts.*
>
> Robinson: *Mr. Rickey, are you looking for a Negro who is afraid to fight back?*

Rickey, exploding: *Robinson,
I'm looking for a ballplayer with
guts enough* not *to fight back.*

Not fighting back would be hard.
Especially in the racially charged climate
of the United States at the time. But
Robinson would not disappoint the man
who gave him a chance.

Robinson's groundbreaking career
didn't begin in the United States —
Robinson got his start in Canada. Rickey
had him play for the Dodgers farm
team, the Montreal Royals. Robinson
faced racism during his season with the
Royals, especially when they toured in the
southern United States. But after a great
first game, Montreal fans supported the
talented player.

Robinson's first MLB game for the
Brooklyn Dodgers was in 1947. It was a
moment that would transform the sport of

Farm Teams

In pro sports, a drafted player doesn't always start playing for the team right away. Teams know that it takes time for someone to get used to playing at a high level. So they send new players to their farm team, a minor-league affiliate (which can be in any city) that develops the players' skills. When the team feels that a player is ready, they call him up to the big league. Even after playing for a pro team, the player can be sent back down to the affiliate team at any time.

baseball — and open the eyes and minds of many. Robinson was hitless, but scored the winning run.

Robinson faced enormous hurdles, from fans and other teams and teammates. The St. Louis Cardinals threatened to strike. Players threw black cats on the field. One of his own teammates started a petition to get Robinson kicked off the team. The Ku Klux Klan — a racist group known to threaten and kill blacks — sent him a death threat. But Robinson kept his cool. And he rose to become a fantastic baseball player.

So it was no wonder that Willie O'Ree, a black baseball player from New Brunswick, turned to Robinson for inspiration.

"He was the bravest man in the world for believing in his dream — and for making it happen," Willie writes.

Imagine not only getting to see your idol, but meeting him. Robinson started talking to Willie and they chatted about baseball and hockey. "But there are no black men playing hockey," Robinson said to Willie.

"I play hockey, Mr. Robinson," 13-year-old Willie said. "And one day, I'll play in the big leagues, too."

Sure enough, seven years later, in 1955, Willie got the chance to play pro

Willie O'Ree with the Marysville Royals baseball team, 1955 New Brunswick champions

baseball. He was playing in the summer for the Marysville Royals, mostly because it provided him with money and was a way of keeping in shape when he wasn't playing hockey. He was approached by a Milwaukee Braves scout. Willie insisted that he wasn't interested in playing pro. Still, the scout convinced him to try out.

The baseball camp was in Waycross, Georgia. The Deep South.

The southern United States was an ar

known for its strong views on race. For many of the people there, blacks were not equals. Segregation, where whites and blacks were separated, was accepted. Black children didn't go to the same schools as white children. Blacks were not allowed to sit at the front of buses. Blacks were not allowed to drink out of the same water fountains as whites. It was a world unlike Canada. It was a world Willie was going to visit.

The first things Willie saw when he entered the airport terminal in Atlanta were signs marking "White Only" and "Colored Only" washrooms.

"I walked into the colored one," he writes. "I wasn't going to cause a revolution during my first few minutes in town."

Willie went out and hailed a cab. He explained to the black cab driver that he needed to stay in a hotel. The cabbie took him to a blacks-only hotel. Willie got the

Rosa Parks

On December 1, 1955, 42-year-old Rosa Parks was heading home from the Montgomery Fair department store where she worked. She sat near the back of the segregated bus, behind the first ten rows reserved for whites. Shortly after Parks took her seat, the bus driver asked her and the three other black passengers to move farther back to make room for white passengers. Rosa Parks refused. She was arrested for refusing to obey a bus driver. Blacks and others fighting for racial equality boycotted the Montgomery buses for 381 days after her arrest. Martin Luther King Jr., who supported non-violent protests, became the spokesperson for the boycott. Rosa Parks's challenge prompted protests across the country, and was one of the most important stands for equal rights in the United States.

message loud and clear. Welcome to th Deep South.

When Willie arrived at camp, he

assigned to a dorm for African-Americans and other people of colour from the West Indies and Cuba.

One Sunday, Willie and his teammates went to church. After the service, they had some time before the bus would pick them up.

"So we started walking down the streets and I was looking for signs for where I could go and where I couldn't go," Willie says. "And they came to this drugstore, and I didn't see any signs. . . . Four or five of the guys that I was with went inside and sat up at the counter and at the end of the counter there were two white gentlemen sitting . . . I was standing just inside the door looking at some postcards. . . . The white gentlemen made racial remarks. So we went outside and we went to the bus top and waited there until the bus picked up.

'I was never used to that treatment and

I just said forget about baseball and just concentrate on hockey."

Outside the dorm where Willie stayed, the coaches put up a list of names. They were the boys who were going home. After the first week, Willie's name wasn't there. He had to admit to himself that he was a bit disappointed. The second week, his name was on the list. Secretly, he was happy.

"They called me into the office and said, 'Mr. O'Ree, we were impressed with your play, but we think you need a little more seasoning, and we're going to send you back home,'" Willie says.

It was a long trip home.

"So, I was on the bus five days," Willie recalls. "Blacks had to sit in the back of the bus. I wasn't accustomed to this, so I got on the bus and started heading north and as I was travelling further north, started moving up in the bus. When I g up to Bangor, Maine, I was sitting at the front of the bus."

Willie was home. And he never looked back.

4 Blindsided

Willie loved hockey. It was a game that made him feel free. It was a game where he could fly. But play pro hockey? It had never really occurred to him . . . not until he was 14 and his brother Richard pointed out to him that his talent and love for the game were obvious.

Richard encouraged Willie about his skills for the game. "You could be the first black man in the NHL," Richa told him. It took some time before W started to believe that he *could* be the first.

Willie was playing for the Fredericton Capitals when he was approached by Phil Watson, former forward for the New York Rangers and Montreal Canadiens. Watson asked Willie to play for the Quebec Frontenacs of the Quebec Junior Hockey League. "You've got the skills and the ability to play in the NHL," he said. But Watson warned Willie that because he was black, he was sure to have a hard time. The key, Watson said, was for Willie to ignore it. It was important that Willie stay in the game and keep his wits about him.

This praise, this advice, was coming from a former NHLer, a Stanley Cup champion. And Willie was listening.

Willie went on to play the 1954–5 season for the Frontenacs. Then he ...yed for the Kitchener–Waterloo Junior ...ucks, a farm team for the Montreal

Canadiens, in the 1955–56 season.

Coach "Blackjack" Stewart told Willie, "You know there hasn't been a black player in the NHL, and you could be the first."

Willie recalls, "It kinda went in one ear and out the other."

One day, the Canucks were playing a game against Guelph. During the game, Willie's teammate took a slapshot from the point. Just as he did, Willie was checked by the other team's defence. Willie turned to find the puck. And find it he did. The puck deflected off a stick and hit him above his right eye.

"It felt as if my head exploded," Willie writes. "When the puck struck me in the eye, I was still conscious. I remember dropping down to the ice and I could fe the blood rushing down my face, and next thing, I'm placed in an ambul and taken to the hospital."

At the hospital, it was obvious that the damage to Willie was very serious. He had a broken nose and a broken cheekbone.

"I'm in the recovery room and Doctor Henderson comes in and there's a patch over my right eye. My left eye was blurry." Willie thought he was blind in his left eye. Willie recalls Dr. Henderson said, "The impact of the puck completely shattered the retina and you're going to be blind. And you'll never play hockey again."

Willie's panic rose. But later the doctor said that the sight would return in the left eye. After a while of straining to see out of his left eye, light started to filter through.

Willie was crushed. And scared. He had no family at his side. He was alone and had just received the worst news of is life. His hockey career was over. The ng he cherished had been snatched y from him by a puck to the eye. How d this be? What would he do?

He called his family and told them of his injury, but he didn't tell them how serious the injury was or that the doctor said he'd never play hockey again. He just couldn't. Even so, his father encouraged him to find another job, something other than hockey. But for Willie, that wasn't an option.

When he was discharged from the hospital, Willie returned home. After a month and a half, he decided to hit the ice, much to the dismay of his mother and father. Returning to the game was a bit harder than Willie had expected. He hadn't lost any of his skills. But every time a puck came near him, he'd flinch. His wounds — both physical and mental — were still healing. What kind of hockey player could he be if he was afraid of th puck? Willie became more determined prove the doctor wrong.

Playing with no helmet or face sh

he was definitely taking a risk. But Willie was never one to back down from a challenge. One of his heroes was goalie Terry Sawchuk. Like Willie, he had been hit in the eye with an puck.

Willie was a left-hand shot and played left wing. Since he was blind in his right eye, he had to turn slightly to the right to see the play from his good eye. This was awkward when he was playing the left side of the ice. He had to slow down. Players who knew he had been injured were making a point of finding him and hitting him.

Milt Schmidt, the coach who would call up O'Ree to play in the NHL, said, "One thing that annoyed me later was that he had only one eye and I knew nothing about it. Not many people knew. If the NHL had known, they'd have never let him play."

Willie worked hard and his teammates ˈ note.

Jim Kyte

Jim Kyte began to lose his hearing when he was just three years old. Like Willie, he refused to let his impairment keep him from the hockey he loved. Kyte hit the ice as a Winnipeg Jet in 1982. He worked hard and became known as a tough guy. But how can you figure out where the puck is going if you can't hear the plays being made? Kyte wore a special helmet to protect his hearing aids. But even with the aids, he couldn't hear the calls his teammates made on the ice. So he would lip-read. And when playing against the boards, he used the glass to figure out who was behind him and what to expect.

"I think it was astonishing that he was able to play at all," Bruins defence Doug Mohns would later say in an interview. "Playing hockey at the highest level tough enough, but playing well with eye is incredible. Good peripheral is so important to a hockey player. I can't imagine how anyone could do what he did. When he shared his secret with me, I was speechless, but I kept my promise that I would not tell anyone, and I never did."

Willie didn't let any of this stop him. He continued to play at his best. And his greatest asset was his speed. He remembers that "skating at the early age and being on the ice as much as I was, I had the ability to be standing still and be at top speed in four or five strides, where other players had to take six or seven strides, and that's where I had the advantage . . . I got a lot of breakaways when I was playing."

Willie finished his final year of junior hockey not knowing what would happen next. He was still a good player, and he knew that. He had played in 41 games with Kitchener and ended up with an impressive goals and 28 assists, for 58 points. But would his injury cripple his career?

At the end of the 1954–55 season, Willie returned home. He was visiting his sister Thelma when there was a knock at the front door. She left to answer it and then returned. "There's a Mr. Imlach here to see you," she said.

It was Punch Imlach. Imlach would go on to be one of the most famous coaches in NHL history, coaching the Toronto Maple Leafs for 13 seasons. But this was many years before that. Then, he was coach of the Quebec Aces of the Quebec Senior Hockey League (QSHL). The Aces were a pro team. They were one step away from the NHL.

Imlach told Willie he wanted to sign him for the Aces. He was putting together a championship team and wanted Willie on it.

This was a big deal for Willie. Imlach was offering $3,500 a year. This was wh a car cost about $2,000; rent might be a month. It wasn't close to the millions that pro athletes make today, but at the time, it was good money.

But Willie knew that the playoffs meant more work. So he said, "Punch, if you're putting together a championship team, that means we're going to get in the playoffs. I want $300 if we get into the playoffs. And more money if I score 20 goals."

Imlach reluctantly agreed.

Willie was going pro.

5 Playing Pro

Willie learned to speak French. He loved living in Quebec. And it was relatively cheap to live there, so Willie could send money to his parents. Willie was able to make a dream come true for his mother.

While Willie was growing up on Charlotte Street, his mother had loved a house down the street. It was the on[e] owned by the Lawrence family, the ot[her] black family in town. Mrs. O'Ree always wanted that house, even th[...]

it was smaller than the one they rented. Willie's mother found out that Mrs. Lawrence was selling her house.

Willie was making over $60 a week, which was plenty enough for him. He could buy groceries and pay his rent, and still have enough money to save. He had enough left over to send some home to his mother to put into a joint bank account. When he found out that Mrs. Lawrence's house was for sale, he told his mother to use the money they'd saved together to buy that house.

"They had always made a home for me," Willie writes about his parents. "A wonderful place that I would go back to in a second if I could time travel. And because of hockey, I could help make a ome for them."

Willie loved hockey, and the Aces — first pro team — were a great team. h Imlach had a reputation of being tough. He was rough and knew what he wanted. And what he wanted was to win. But Willie never had a problem with him. He knew Imlach was a driven man and he respected that. After all, he wanted to win, too.

The Aces had a great reputation. They had turned out players like Jean Béliveau, who went on to play for the powerhouse Montreal Canadiens.

Also on that team was Herb Carnegie. Most young people today have never heard of Herb Carnegie, but he was an incredible player — an incredible *black* player.

Willie had a great season with the Aces, finishing with 22 goals and 12 assists. The Aces finished an amazing 13 points ahead of the second-place team, the Chicouti Saguenéens, winning 40 of their 68 gar The Aces made the playoffs and the Duke of Edinburgh title. Wl

Herb Carnegie

Many people call Herb Carnegie the best player *never* to have played in the NHL. Born in 1919 in Toronto, Ontario, Carnegie was a great player. He played for the Sherbrooke Saints of the Quebec Provincial Hockey League, on a line with his brother Ossie and Matty McIntyre (who was also black). There, Carnegie won the MVP award for three years in a row. In 1948, he won the league's scoring title with 127 points. That year, the New York Rangers told Carnegie to report to their training camp in Saranac Lake, New York. During his first week of camp, he was offered $2,700 to play for the Rangers's lowest-level farm team in Tacoma, Washington. But Carnegie was being paid $5,100 to play in Sherbrooke. He turned down the offer. The Rangers made two other offers, the final one for $4,700 a year, to play for their top farm team in New Haven, Connecticut. Carnegie continued to refuse. Carnegie said he couldn't take a 00 pay cut. He needed to support his ily. In doing so, he may have missed out reaking the colour barrier in the NHL ars before Willie O'Ree.

incredible first season Willie had! For him, it was as if he'd won the Stanley Cup. He couldn't help but think that he'd proven the doctor in Guelph wrong. He was sure to make it to the NHL, right?

But the road to the NHL was a long and hard one. Even if you were white, the competition was tough. There were only six NHL teams at the time, so there weren't many spots available. You couldn't be a good hockey player. You had to be a great hockey player. And though Willie was great, he had a strike against him most of his teammates didn't — he was black.

Fans in Quebec City were great, but it wasn't that way everywhere. Willie recalls that the toughest place to play was Chicoutimi, in the province of Quebec.

Willie played with Stan Maxwell, another black player, but Stan was fair skinned. Willie was dark skinned. Whenever the team went to Chicoutimi,

Willie O'Ree played his first professional season with the Quebec Aces

Willie was faced with insults and taunts. They would call him *maudit negre,* which could be translated as "damned nigger."

"There were remarks from players and fans, but I let it go in one ear and out the other. I learned . . . from a young age that names will never hurt you unless you let them. My brother just said, 'Willie, just be proud of who you are . . . if people can't accept you for the individual you are, then it's their tough luck.'"

So Willie ignored the taunts. Until one day when he couldn't.

Willie was in the penalty box. Back then, there wasn't any glass separating the box from the fans.

The chants started while Willie was sitting in the box. At first he ignored them, as usual. But as the chanting grew louder, he knew something was different. He could tell by the noise that someone was coming down to the box.

As the Chicoutimi fan approached the box, Willie leaped up and clocked him with one punch.

Chicoutimi fans started to swarm the box. Willie's teammates rushed to defend him. It was an ugly situation.

Sadly, Willie often faced the cruel taunts of small-minded hockey fans and players. What they couldn't see was what many of the players could: that Willie was fast and that he was a good player.

There were players who would charge him and try to throw him off his game. But Willie didn't take it sitting down. He always stood up for himself. In his first season, he had 80 penalty minutes over 68 games. It wasn't because he enjoyed fighting: in fact, he hated it. He thought it made him lower himself to the level of his attackers. But he also wasn't about to give up or let them push him around.

"I never fought one time because of

racial remarks," he said in a TV interview years later. "I fought because guys buttended me and speared me and crossed-checked me.... I fought because I had to, not because I wanted to."

6 First Taste of the NHL

It was the summer of 1957 and Willie had come off his incredible first pro season with the Aces. He was back in Fredericton, working during the day at a service station. One day, he came home from work to find a letter from the Boston Bruins waiting for him. Not only was it from the Bruins, but it was from General Manager Lester Patrick.

Dear Bill,
The Boston Bruins will hold
their training camp here in
Boston at the Boston Garden.
We will begin our training
period on the afternoon of
Sunday, September 15. We
would like you to report to the
Manger Hotel in Boston before
noon on September 15.

Willie was more than thrilled. He was invited to training camp for an NHL team! And the importance of the moment didn't get past him: there were no other black players in the league. He could very well be the first black man to play in the NHL, just like his brother Richard had said.

Boston was a fantastic team to pla
for. They had won three Stanley Cu
and were battling the Canadiens as
of the top teams in the league. The

had great players like Milt Schmidt, who became a Bruins coach, and had fantastic newcomers like Bronco Horvath and Johnny Bucyk.

Willie's friend Stan Maxwell, the other black player on the Aces, received the letter, too. They set out for Boston together.

At training camp, the rookies and veterans trained together. The old-timers were great and encouraged Willie and Stan. Willie ran the drills, did the sit-ups, and gave it his all in camp. When the time came to choose the team, the managers told Willie he had talent, but that he needed a bit more "seasoning." Unlike the time he was cut at baseball camp for the Milwaukee Braves, Willie was disappointed. But he knew that he'd given it his all. He couldn't have changed anything. And he felt, deep down, that be back.

O'Ree in the Boston Bruins dressing room

Back Willie went to the Quebec Aces. But he wasn't there for very much longer.

In 1958, during the same season, he got a phone call from Boston. The Bruins had some injured players and needed Willie to play.

Bruins coach Milt Schmidt later said that Willie being black had nothing to do with his being called up. All Schm cared about was whether or not W was a good player. "Willie was a very good skater, one of the fastest in the NHL," Schmidt says. "At times, it seemed his legs went faster than he could think."

So Willie headed to his first NHL game in Montreal, a place he knew well. And he also knew the Montreal Forum. He'd played on that ice with the Aces. But this time, it felt different. It was a new day, a day when Willie would step onto the ice and make history. He was the first black man to play in an NHL game. Thousands of people would read about it. Maybe black boys would be inspired. Maybe they would see that they, too, could join the ranks of the best hockey players in the world.

The date was Saturday, January 18, 1958. "The lights were brighter," Willie writes. "And the ice was brighter. The ns seemed more elegant and nobody led me any names."

nd when he pulled on the brown and

gold sweater, it was the biggest thrill of his life.

Willie's coach Milt Schmidt knew that it was an historic occasion. He sat Willie down and told him the whole Bruins organization knew the meaning of that night.

Years later, Willie's teammate Bronco Horvath said of that night, "We told him, 'don't worry, you'll be fine. If anyone hits you, slurs you or tries to hurt you, there'll be nine guys on him in the blink of an eye.'"

"The colour of a person's skin was never an issue in hockey," former Boston defence Fern Flaman recalled. "This was a case of the player deserved an opportunity to have a chance to come up and play the NHL. There were so few black pla playing hockey at that time. At that in Canada, black athletes were common in ball sports. Willie w

O'Ree takes to the ice during practice with the Bruins

hockey player to us."

Willie O'Ree was the first black man to
ay in the National Hockey League. He
the Jackie Robinson of hockey. He
e down a barrier that had stood since
gue was formed in 1917.

was just a fast skater and I remember

66

he was very happy to have made it to the NHL, like all kids were at that time," Flaman says. "He fit right in with everybody and everybody liked him. I know I've read where he heard insults from the crowds, but on that occasion, he got a big hand when he was introduced."

Horvath remembers Willie's ability to skate: "I told Willie, if you die, leave me your legs. Willie's legs and my body? I'd have made them forget the Rocket. From a standstill, Willie could take off flying, no one could catch him. His jersey used to billow out behind him."

Though the Canadiens seemed unbeatable, Boston won 3–0 that night. Willie didn't have any points on the board, but that didn't matter to him. H flew down the ice using his legend speed. He went into corners and w afraid to go hard after the puck.

"There was nothing said abou

O'Ree breaking the colour barrier, or being the first of his race to play in the National Hockey League," Willie says. "But it didn't really dawn on me until the next day. I was just happy to play with the Bruins and be on the winning team that night."

Willie went on to play a second game in Boston the next day. His parents were there to watch the game. The Bruins lost 6–2, and again Willie didn't get any points. But it didn't matter to him. He had realized a dream.

Willie was always good at being true to himself. He never let anyone dissuade him from playing the game he loved. And all that persistence paid off. He was among the biggest names in hockey. The only question was, would he be able to stay, or would the racism that plagued me take its toll?

e was sent back down after those

The Bruins–Canadiens Rivalry

The Boston Bruins and Montreal Canadiens — also known as *Les Habitants*, or the Habs — have played against each other for almost as long as the NHL has been around. By 2012, the two teams had met more than 600 times, and in the post-season, the Habs won 24 of 32 series. From the mid-1950s to the late 1960s, the Habs enjoyed a particularly successful run, bringing home five Stanley Cups in a row and nine between 1955 and 1969. But the two teams have one of the most intense rivalries in any pro sport.

two games, but he knew he'd be back. He just knew it.

7 Getting Back to Boston

After his two games with the Bruins, Willie was sure that they'd call him back. He may not have scored any points, but he'd shown them his best.

Willie's confidence was rewarded when he was invited to attend training camp the next summer. So once again, he and Stan Maxwell headed back to Boston.

It was nice to be among familiar faces, doing familiar drills. Once again, Willie gave it his all. Willie believed he'd make the cut this time, but he was wrong. He was disappointed, but he didn't give up.

That season Willie played for the Springfield Indians in the American Hockey League (AHL). The coach and general manager of the team was Eddie Shore, a former Boston Bruins defenceman. He was born of grit, having worked hard on a farm as a young man. He hadn't shown much of an interest in hockey as a boy, and his siblings teased him about it. Determined to prove them wrong, he ended up one of the hardest players in his era. And he was tough. By the end of his time as a player, he had broken his nose 14 times and had 978 stitches.

Shore's toughness carried through in his coaching career. Other coaches would send problem players to him. But to many, Shore seemed unstable. He was renowned for doing off-the-wall things, like making the team practice in the dark to save electricity. He was unpredictable and hard to work with. Willie didn't like Shore, and Shore didn't like Willie. It wasn't a race issue, but a personality issue. The first five games of the season, Willie sat on the bench. When he was finally put on the ice to replace an injured player, Willie got on to the ice and tripped. Shore sent him back to the Aces. Willie was happy to go, even though he felt that Shore's decision was unfair. After all, Shore hadn't even seen him play in a game.

Willie played for the Quebec Aces for the rest of the 1957–58 season and then the 1958–59 season as well. The season after that, he played for the Kingston Frontenacs. There, he had his best pro season, with 21 goals and 25 assists. Willie was doing what he loved and he was doing it well — all the while with just one good eye.

While in Kingston, Willie met his first

girlfriend, Lynn Campbell, after a hockey game. But Lynn was white. At this time, mixed couples weren't common. Those who were in these relationships faced hardships and severe racism.

It wasn't just about white people not accepting black people. It also worked the other way around. Many blacks distrusted whites. In fact, Willie's parents weren't happy about him dating Lynn. They were worried about what other people would think. They were worried that the couple would be hurt or, as had happened in the United States, even killed.

Willie figured that it didn't matter who he dated. But he had always been very close to his family. How they felt *did* matter to him.

After his season ended, Willie wa home. He decided to pay Lynn a visit Kingston and invited his mother to cc along. But it was obvious that she w happy about the relationship. Because of this, Willie ended it with Lynn.

Willie played with the Hull-Ottawa Canadiens of the short-lived Eastern Professional Hockey League during the 1960–61 season. Sure, he was hoping to make it back to the NHL one day, but he was happy giving it his all for the Canadiens.

Willie might have had just one good eye, but it wasn't stopping him. He was able to perform as good as, and even better than, many of his fellow players. And he knew that the NHL couldn't find out about his loss of sight. He hadn't taken the League's sight test when he played the two games for Boston. If they found out he couldn't see, it would mean the end of dream for him. The league required 100 r cent vision.

n December 1960, Willie once again call from Boston. He was ecstatic.

He headed back to Boston and stayed with his cousin just outside the city in Roxbury.

To Willie's surprise, the media didn't make a big deal about him playing. He wished they would pay attention to his achievement. He wanted to inspire black boys who might think it was impossible to make a career of their love of hockey.

Boston defence Doug Mohns recalls, "As a hockey player, he was a fast skater, quick on his feet, and he worked hard at both ends of the ice, which not all players did. How could you help but admire the guy?"

But while staying with his cousin, Willie was at least able to inspire children and others in that neighbourhood. Roxbury was an area where many blacks lived. Willie would hand out tickets to Bruins games when he could. He was the first black man in the NHL. This was monumental to the community. Neighbourhood kids would head to the games and cheer him on. Sometimes Willie's brother Richard would attend. Willie proudly wore his sweater with 22 on the back and gave them a show.

Being in the NHL was a dream come true for Willie. He loved to travel and he loved playing against the stars of the game. Gordie Howe, known as "Mr. Hockey," was an amazing inspiration. Howe had a powerful shot and was a great physical player. Most of all, Howe was already acting as role model and ambassador for the sport that Willie loved so much.

On January 1, 1961, the Bruins were hosting the Habs at Boston Garden in a tough game. The Habs had won their fifth consecutive Stanley Cup the season before, and looked hard to beat.

Boston was ahead of Montreal with a score of 2–1 midway through the third

O'Ree on the ice during a game against the Toronto Maple Leafs

period. Willie took a pass from Leo Boivin. He sped by Habs defence Jean-Guy Talbot. A Habs player broke his stick

The Bruins: One of the Original Six

People will talk about an NHL team being part of the "Original Six." The Original Six teams were the Toronto Maple Leafs, Montreal Canadiens, Boston Bruins, Detroit Red Wings, Chicago Black Hawks, and New York Rangers. The nickname is a bit misleading, as the league formed in 1917 with only two of these teams: the Canadiens and the Maple Leafs. Over the years, teams came and went. After the NHL expanded to a total of 12 teams in 1967, the nickname was given to separate the "originals" from the new ones. To this day, these teams are regarded as powerhouses in the NHL, producing some of the best players. Some Bruins legends include Eddie Shore, Phil Esposito, Cam Neely, Ray Bourque, and, most notably, Bobby Orr, who many think is one of the best players to ever take to the ice.

trying to stop him. Willie flew past them both. In front of goalie Charlie Hodge, he fired a low shot. The red light was on. Willie had just netted his first NHL goal!

The crowd rose to their feet and cheered for a full two minutes. Willie's goal ended up being the winning goal as Boston defeated Montreal 3–2.

"I can still recall the great applause I got from scoring that first goal," Willie says. He cherishes that puck to this day.

After scoring his first NHL goal, Willie found that Boston fans really did support him. It was a welcome feeling. Especially since not everyone felt that way about him. And it could get tough on the ice.

"In the penalty box, you know, stuff would be thrown . . . they'd spit on me," he recalled years later.

One such ugly experience sticks with him.

Willie was set to play against Chicago.

The Black Hawks had their share of stars, with players like Stan Mikita and Bobby Hull. As much as Willie was an NHL player, he was still a fan. Willie couldn't wait to see his heroes play.

But it wasn't to be.

Two minutes into the game at Chicago Stadium, Chicago right-wing Eric Nesterenko skated up to Willie and muttered, "Nigger." Willie wasn't one to take abuse, but he knew when to fight and when not to. If he had dropped his gloves every time he heard a racial slur, he would have had no ice time. But Nesterenko carried it further. He butt-ended Willie with his stick, knocking out two of his teeth. Then he tried to high-stick Willie, again calling him "nigger." Willie avoided the stick, but came back up and brought his stick down on Nesterenko's head. This was a fight he was ready to take on.

Players from both benches flooded the

ice. It was a bench-clearing brawl. Fans, thinking Willie had been the instigator, were enraged. Willie was taken off the ice into the dressing room to be treated for his injuries. And that's where he stayed. Officials said that they were worried for Willie's safety.

"There wasn't any TV . . . I sat alone wondering what was happening out on the ice. So much for seeing Bobby Hull and Stan Mikita and Glenn Hall," Willie writes. "I was a prisoner in Chicago Stadium."

In an article in *USA Today* years later, he would recall that he thought about quitting at that moment. But then he reconsidered.

"Right there and then, I made a decision: No, I'm not quitting," he said. "If I am going to leave this league, it will be because my skills aren't good enough. I'm not going to leave because someone is

trying to drive me out of the league."
So Willie stayed right where he was.

8 Fighting Till the End

Willie played in 43 games for the Bruins during their 70-game season. He had four goals and ten assists. Not a bad tally for his first real go in the NHL.

So when the 1960–61 season was over, he was optimistic. General Manager Lester Patrick and Coach Milt Schmidt told him that they'd liked what they'd seen. They told him to enjoy his summer and expect to return the following season.

Years later, Schmidt would say, "He

always had a smile, no matter what was happening, and he was a very brainy player, always highly regarded by his teammates and the higher-ups."

So Willie went home and shared the news with his family, who were as happy as he was. He was going to be a regular in the NHL!

Except that's not how things played out for him.

One day Willie received a call from a reporter for a local newspaper. He asked Willie how he felt about being traded to Montreal. *What?* Willie thought. He'd been traded to the Montreal Canadiens — the star-studded Canadiens! His heart sank. Even if the Canadiens organization acquired him, the best he could hope for was to play for their farm team. There was no way he'd play in the NHL for the Habs.

Willie felt betrayed. The Bruins had told him to expect to be back and they

O'Ree was disappointed to discover he would not continue to play for the Bruins the following season

traded him? Why? He would never find out.

As he expected, instead of playing for the Montreal Canadiens, Willie played for their farm team, the Hull-Ottawa Canadiens. Ironically, it was the team he had been playing for when Boston had called him up.

On November 12, 1961, Willie showed up for practice with the Canadiens, just before 8:30 a.m. He was told that General Manager Sam Pollack wanted to see him immediately. Pollack told Willie that he'd been traded to the Los Angeles Blades of the Western Hockey League (WHL). *Does Los Angeles even have a hockey team?* Willie wondered. This had to be a mistake.

But it wasn't. He was handed a plane ticket. His flight left in four hours.

As far as Willie was concerned, he was headed as far away from the NHL as possible. It was a crushing blow. But being a hockey player meant he had little control over where he ended up. So once again,

Willie went where his hockey career was taking him.

When he arrived at his hotel, he bumped into Jean-Marc Picard, who he'd played against in junior hockey. It was a relief to see a familiar face. The following season, Stan Maxwell joined the team.

California agreed with Willie. And Willie liked California. The fans were fantastic. In fact, more fans showed up for Blades games than they did for the games in Quebec. In his first season, Willie scored 28 goals and 26 assists.

Willie started to settle in well. He met Berna Deanne Plummer while on the road in Portland, Oregon. Soon after, they married in Fredericton and had two sons, Kevin and Darren. Willie was often on the road, and would later regret not spending more time with his boys as they grew up.

Although the LA fans were gr

The Watts Riots

In 1965, there were five days of riots in the Watts neighbourhood of Los Angeles, after a young black man was pulled over by a police officer who believed he was drunk. He protested and the police used physical force to arrest him. Crowds gathered and the unrest grew over the next few days. Thirty-four people died and more than 1,000 people were injured; more than 3,400 people were arrested.

wasn't always great on the road. Willie still faced taunts and calls of "nigger."

In the 1964–65 season, the team got a new coach. Coach Alf Pike, who had found out about Willie's right eye, put him on right wing. The change in position took advantage of Willie's sighted and improved his already skilful play. He upped his scoring to 38 goals and sts.

And then a promising development: Los Angeles was given an NHL team in the league's expansion. Willie was certain that he'd play for the new team. After all, he'd proven himself on the Blades, right?

But this was a very difficult time for blacks in the United States. There were riots and protests as blacks struggled to battle racism and achieve rights equal to those of white people.

Instead of being called up by the NHL, Willie was called by the San Diego Gulls of the WHL. They were struggling and hoped that the addition of Willie would help their team. Willie wasn't too sure. He was 32. He didn't know how much hockey he had left in him. But he decided to sign. In the 1968–69 season, he we on to win the scoring title.

By that time, Willie was dive from Berna. He had met a woman, Deljeet, who was of Sou

O'Ree with his son and daughter and neighbours in San Diego, California

background, and fallen in love. They
married, even though her family wasn't
appy that she was marrying outside of
race. Racism wasn't only between
s and whites.

Gulls loaned out Willie for part
1972–73 season to Connecticut,

to play for the New Haven Nighthawks of the AHL. And that's when Willie witnessed of some of the most horrible racism he'd ever seen.

Sure, Willie had been called names. He'd been treated harshly. But if he thought heading back east would mean facing less racism, he would soon learn that he couldn't escape prejudice. Even after a decade of civil unrest and race riots, things hadn't changed completely.

Willie played games on the road. Some places he played in were better than others. Virginia was not one of them. While on the ice, he would hear people yell out, "Why aren't you out picking cotton?" One day, someone actually threw a black cat onto the ice. The poor thing w stunned. Willie went out to pick it and he and the cat were more than when the game was over.

The racism continued even

east coast. While he was playing in Baltimore, Maryland, he was forbidden from entering a restaurant where he was meeting teammates. Once he tried to rent a cottage, but when the real estate agent saw him, she suddenly told him that it had been rented. This was in 1973. How could discrimination still be going on? This was what so many people had fought — and even died — to end. Although strides had been made, change was slow.

When Willie returned to San Diego, he played the rest of the season and then one more. But in 1974 he retired. He was tired of all the travelling that hockey demanded. He was almost 40 years old, after all. And he also wanted to spend more time with his new wife.

But Willie didn't stay retired long. He out of retirement to play 53 more with the San Diego Hawks in the Coast Hockey League, where he

NHL Expansion

Initially the NHL consisted of six teams. But the league knew that with more teams came more money. It was also fearful that a rival hockey league would compete for the Stanley Cup. So in 1967, the league added six more teams: the California Seals, Los Angeles Kings, Minnesota North Stars, Philadelphia Flyers, Pittsburgh Penguins, and St. Louis Blues. Over the years, the League continued to expand. By 1979, it consisted of 21 teams (having absorbed some teams from a rival league). The NHL continued to expand until it reached the 30 teams it has today.

scored 21 goals and 25 assists.

Finally Willie had had enough. Deljeet was pregnant. This time, he planned to be home for his child. This time, he would watch his son or daughter grow up.

9 A Voice for Many

Willie O'Ree had smashed the colour barrier in the NHL.

Or had he?

In 1996, Bryant McBride came up with an idea. McBride was the vice president of business development for the NHL and also worked on the NHL's Diversity Task Force. He wanted to

Hockey Is for Everyone

The NHL has taken steps to fix the lack of black, Asian, and other minority players in the league. The NHL's Diversity Task Force was started in 1995 as a way of encouraging children from other cultures and financial backgrounds to play hockey. The Task Force's Hockey Is For Everyone program provides support for not-for-profit hockey leagues for children in Canada and the United States. It specifically supports children who might otherwise not have the money to play hockey. There are over 30 programs in North America; over 45,000 boys and girls have participated.

invite 24 children from various ethnic communities to participate in a hockey tournament in Boston. He wanted to call it the Willie O'Ree All-Star Weekend. He called Willie to tell him and ask him if he'd come out for the first tournament.

"I was surprised and flattered," Willie

writes in his autobiography. "Imagine an All-Star Weekend for minority kids, and one named after me. It's something I never dreamed could happen."

Although Willie was working as a security guard for the San Diego Chargers of the National Football League, he took time off to attend. It also was the NHL's All-Star Weekend, so it allowed him to see some of the players from his time in hockey. But it didn't end there. Willie also attended other functions promoting hockey to troubled kids.

The next year, Willie was asked to attend the Willie O'Ree All-Star Weekend again. The following year, after the NHL All-Star Weekend, Bryant asked Willie if he'd be willing to work for the Diversity Task Force permanently. What better spokesperson could they have than Willie O'Ree? Willie was appointed the program's director.

Willie was pleased to finally be front and centre promoting diversity within the NHL. He had always wanted to be a source of hope to black youths. Now the NHL was giving him a voice as ambassador for the Task Force's Hockey Is for Everyone program.

"We won't turn a boy or girl away who wants to play," he says. "I speak at a number of schools — elementary, middle schools, junior high, high schools — and the first message is education. Staying in school. Setting goals for yourselves. Believing in yourself and feeling good about yourself."

Willie relishes the opportunity to encourage children all over North America. He jumps at the chance to use himself and his career as an example.

"My message is if you think you can, you can; if you think you can't, you' right . . . I use my example when

Willie O'Ree continues to be an inspiration to young minority hockey players

doctor told me that I would never play hockey again because I was blind in my right eye," he says. "But he didn't know about my goals and my dreams and how ‾ felt inside . . . You can do anything you t your mind to, but you have to believe yourself. Don't let anybody tell you

you can't obtain your goal."

While it's encouraging to see the NHL try to expose boys and girls to hockey, not everyone is as open-minded as the league. Over the past several years, Willie has received threats in the mail.

"I still have the letters," O'Ree said in a *USA Today* interview in 2008. "They said, 'We know there are players of your kind in Canada, but you don't need to bring them to the States.' They said they knew what to do with my kind."

Willie is disappointed that this kind of racism has endured for all these years. But it hasn't stopped him from supporting the children in the communities who have shown an interest in the game.

William McCants, the Detroit Hockey Association's co-founder, acknowledged Willie's role in the NHL in 2008: "H may be more important now than he back then because today he is reac the kids. Back then what he did went unnoticed."

Although Willie O'Ree may not have seen his influence while he was playing in the NHL, others did notice. He was able to inspire other young black players.

"It always meant a lot to me and was powerful to me to be able to look and see how many black players were in the NHL," says Calgary Flames star Jarome Iginla.

Willie's role in the NHL has been acknowledged all across Canada and the United States. In his hometown of Fredericton, there is a hockey rink that bears his name. In 1984, he was inducted into the New Brunswick Sports Hall of Fame. In 2003, he was honoured with the Lester Patrick Award for outstanding service to hockey in the United States. He was also inducted into the San Diego Hall of Champions in 2008. And in 2005, he received the Order of New Brunswick, an incredible honour. But his highest honour came in 2010, when he received the Order of Canada.

"At the heart of all the storms weathering humanity and all the uncertainty bombarding the world, there are women and men reviving hope," said the Right Honourable Michaëlle Jean, the governor General of Canada at the time. "The people we are celebrating today are of that same calibre."

"I was totally surprised...I had butterflies in my stomach. It was a great honour and a great thrill for me," Willie said with his usual sense of humility. "I was overwhelmed. I don't know how my name came up, whether I was nominated by an individual or a group. I was at a loss for words. What an honour."

Perhaps it was NHL Commissioner Gary Bettman who best summarized career and character of Willie O'Ree. Acknowledging Willie's contribution to the NHL, Bettman said that "he has a resolve and an inner strength that allows him to do what he believes and not let anything get in his way."

Epilogue

Although the NHL has made steps to appeal to minorities and underprivileged youths, hockey still continues to experience its share of racist incidents.

During the hockey lockout in 2004–05, Anson Carter, a black hockey player from Toronto, had a banana thrown at him while playing in Russia. It was a reminder that, along with other racial terms, black had been called "monkeys" in the past.

Kevin Weekes, a former NHL p

and now ambassador for the NHL's Diversity Task Force, also had a banana tossed at him, but in North America. It was during the 2002 playoffs in Montreal while he was in goal for the Carolina Hurricanes.

As recently as 2011, in a game against the Detroit Red Wings, Philadelphia Flyers Wayne Simmonds — a black player from Toronto — was taking his shot in a shootout. As he skated down the ice, a banana was thrown. (He still managed to score.)

"I don't know if it had anything to do with the fact I'm black," Simmonds said. "I certainly hope not. When you're black, you kind of expect [racist] things. You learn to deal with it."

The fan would later turn himself in ⸱d say that he didn't understand what ⸱wing a banana meant. But for some, ⸱is hard to believe.

In 2003, former Florida Panthers goalie John Vanbiesbrouck had to resign as coach of the Ontario Hockey League's Sault Greyhounds after he called team captain Trevor Daley "nigger."

In 2012, the Stanley Cup playoffs were marked by another racial incident. In the first round of the playoffs, Joel Ward scored the winning goal for the Washington Capitals as they eliminated the Boston Bruins. Twitter was filled with racist tweets complaining about a black player eliminating the Bruins, calling him "nigger." The irony that the racist tweets were by fans of the Boston Bruins was not lost on some people. They were upset that the team that broke the colour barrier by playing Willie O'Ree could have such ignorant fans.

Ward said that he was shocked by the reaction. "I knew there'd be some ang fans probably, but it's just sad to see," said in a newspaper interview.

But his mother wasn't so surprised. "All his life coming up, it was always some kind of racial remarks with him and hockey," she said. She said that she remembers one time a referee called him "monkey."

Although these incidents have occurred, it hasn't discouraged black youths from pursuing hockey as a career. In 2011, for the first time in the Ontario Hockey League draft, four of the twelve top players chosen were black. It's a sign that times are changing.

"To me that's encouraging," Anson Carter said.

Indeed it is. And it all started with Willie O'Ree.

Author's Note

I was born in 1972. I used to think that my birth occurred at a time of racial tolerance and acceptance. I realize now how naïve I was. It wasn't until I started writing this book that it occurred to me how close I had come to being raised in a completely different time. If I'd been born just ten years earlier, I would have lived in a time that saw inspiration from the Washington March and Martin Luther King Jr.'s "I Have a Dream" speech. I would have lived in a time that saw the Watts race riots in California, a time of persistent racial segregation in the southern United States, a time of the murders of civil rights workers in Mississippi.

My mother is Guyanese and my fath[er] is Italian. Although people were alw[ays] curious about my heritage, I never experienced racism until I was ab[out] years old. I was chatting with a co-worker on Front Street in Toronto when a passerby called me "monkey." I was stunned into silence, and started shaking. I was angry. I was hurt. Later the tears would flow. But it shouldn't have mattered to me what a complete stranger — narrow-minded and ignorant — called me. I knew who I was and was proud to be of mixed heritage. Yet those words stung me, made my chest ache. Words are powerful weapons that can tear through you, down to the bone.

So it is with wonder that I read about accomplishments by people like Rosa Parks, Martin Luther King Jr., Jackie Robinson, and Willie O'Ree. I am extremely grateful for their contributions and their courage. I'd like to say that, that time, faced with the possibility being beaten or even killed, I would made such brave leaps to achieve y. But I'm not sure I would have.

It takes great courage and inner strength to stand up for what you believe in, to try to change where history has placed you or what constraints have been put upon you. So, thank you to those brave black men and women who came before me and allowed me sit anywhere I want on a bus, drink from any water fountain, and pursue any career I chose. Your sacrifices have made my world a better place.

— Nicole Mortillaro, 2012

Glossary

Amateur: a player who is not paid over basic living expenses

Boycott: to stop buying or using something

Called up: when an athlete is brought up from a farm team to play on a major league team

Deep South: an area in the United States that includes Alabama, Georgia, Louisiana, Mississippi, North Carolina, South Carolina, and all or part of Florida, Virginia, Tennessee, Arkansas, and Texas

Emancipation: freeing someone from the control of someone else

Instigator: someone who starts something

Jubilee: a time or program of special events that honours something

Ku Klux Klan: an extremist right-wing secret society that formed in the southern United States; the group aims to suppress the powers of black people and are known for torturing and even murdering blacks

Not-for-profit (business): a company that uses its earnings to operate without profit

Petition: a formal written request that is signed by many people that appeals to an authority for a particular cause

Professional: a player who receives a salary

Rivalries: competition for the same goal

Seasoning: a term used to refer to players who need to sharpen their skills, usually done in the minor leagues or on farm teams

Segregation: the action of setting someone apart from other people

Underground Railroad: a system in place between 1840–60 that help black fugitive slaves escape into Can

Acknowledgements

Special thanks to Willie O'Ree for taking the time to speak with me, and to Rob Wooley of the NHL and Eustace King.

Sources

The Autobiography of Willie O'Ree: Hockey's Black Pioneer, Willie O'Ree, Somerville House Publishing, 2000.

Black Ice: The Lost History of the Colored Hockey League of the Maritimes, 1895–1925, George and Darril Fosty, Nimbus Publishing Limited, 2008

Hockey: A People's History, Michael McKinley, McClelland & Stewart Ltd., 2006

Canada's Sports Hall of Fame

The Hockey Hall of Fame

osa and Raymond Parks Institute for
elf Development (www.rosaparks.org)

Acknowledgements

www.nhl.com

www.espn.com

www.tsn.com

www.usatoday.com, "Willie O'Ree still blazing way in NHL 50 years later," Kevin Allen

www.thecanadianencyclopedia.com

www.pbs.org

About the Author

Nicole Mortillaro is a sports books editor and writer. Her first book in the Recordbooks series was *Something to Prove*, a biography of hockey player Bobby Clarke, who had to defy stereotypes to earn a spot in the NHL. She has also written books on weather for children, and astronomy for adults. Nicole is a first-generation Canadian born to a Guyanese mother and an Italian father. She lives in Toronto, Ontario.

Photo Credits

We gratefully acknowledge the following sources for permission to reproduce the images in this book.

Hockey Hall of Fame: front cover (bottom) and p. 66
Jamie Kellner, copyright 2012: p. 98
National Hockey League: p. 63, 77, 85
New Brunswick Sports Hall of Fame: p. 35, 56
Nova Scotia Archives: front cover (top) and p. 16
Provincial Archives of New Brunswick (York Sunbury Historical Society II collection: P132-121): p. 22
Rick Capetto: p. 90

Index